Sculpture, Prayer and Scripture

Liz Culling

Tutor and Lecturer in Spirituality, Cranmer Hall, Durham

Toddy Hoare

Curate-in-charge, Hillside Parishes, North Yorkshire

Sculptor

GROVE BOOKS LIMITED

RIDLEY HALL RD CAMBRIDGE CB3 9HU

Contents

The Cover Illustration is by Toddy Hoare (see p 24 for title and description)

First Impression November 2004
ISSN 0262-799X
ISBN 1 85174 578 5

Introduction: God the Sculptor 1

When God 'formed man from the dust of the ground' (Gen 2.7) surely he was a sculptor?

Imagine God creating the world for a moment. Read again Genesis 1 and 2. Is God not totally engaged in his great and mysterious project? Is not this a supreme artist at work? 'Formed' suggests a very hands-on approach. Man was shaped, sculpted from the dust of the ground and then life was breathed into him.

There is a wonderful story by Trevor Dennis called 'God's delight' about the creation of the world. The story begins with God busy fashioning the kangaroo.

> He could not quite get the jump right. The poor creature kept on landing on its head. He made the tail a little longer and thicker. 'Now try,' he said. The animal tried. God clapped his hands. 'Perfect!' he cried. 'Let's go and show the angels!'[1]

This story, along with others in the same book, is a reminder of the mystery, the wonder, the infinite variety and the sheer joy of God's creativity.

More seriously, the creation stories remind us that God is concerned with matter. As George MacLeod, leader of the Iona Community, put it in the twentieth century, 'Matter matters to God.' Christians too often overlook our very earthiness in our concern with eternal things. Bishop Tom Wright, in his writings, has been at pains to make it clear that our physicality will go on mattering beyond this present world.[2] God will transform this present created order into something new, just as a seed grows into a plant (1 Cor 15.35ff).

With God the sculptor there is the possibility of re-creation in this present world too

But with God the sculptor there is the possibility of re-creation in this present world too. In Jeremiah 18 we read about the potter who shaped a vessel which was spoiled. Since the clay was malleable, it responded to the potter's hands and was reworked into something good and useful. God is ready to re-shape

Artists have a particular way of seeing the world, and they invite us to see it in a new way for ourselves

our lives. He can remake us if we are prepared to become clay in the potter's hands, responding not resisting. Prayer and Scripture are part of this process.

Artists have a particular way of seeing the world, and they invite us to see it in a new way for ourselves. Their awareness of the world around them can stimulate our own. For example, most of us would not give a line of factory workers trudging down the street a second glance, but the paintings of R S Lowry immortalized the workers of Salford and made us look in a new way. He painted what he saw, but with the awareness of an artist, and thereby captured something of the essence of what it means to be human. Art enables us to see more clearly and more deeply, and so enables us to become better in touch with reality and also with God, who is in all things, beautiful or otherwise.

This booklet has emerged from working with people who wanted to explore the Scriptures and prayer in new and different ways. Much of the material is the result of quiet days with parish groups who came together to explore prayer using sculpture.

Why Use Sculpture as Part of Bible Study and Prayer?

The aim of using sculpture for prayer and Bible study is to open up a variety of possibilities which could help us to focus on Scripture in new and imaginative ways. The bronze figures are intended to be a stimulus towards doing our own Bible study and providing themes for prayer. Some basic knowledge of the Bible is required, but not as much as we might think. With the help of a concordance or Bible dictionary we can follow through themes which strike us as we look closely at the sculpture. We might also be surprised at how much we already know. Knowledge of Scripture is receding in our culture, but there are still many sayings and images in common parlance which originate there. It may be a surprise to find things in Scripture of which we were previously unaware, but that is the whole point. Sittting down with the Bible in our hand and roving through its pages trying to use our own faculties and insights as our guide is an opportunity to get to know it better.

We are two parish priests, a married couple, who are trying to pray and to help others to pray in a busy world where it is difficult to make space to allow the Scriptures to grip us and enter our imagination afresh. Toddy is a trained sculptor who says he prefers to preach in bronze. He would claim to be a Prayer Book Anglican, someone for whom the words of the *Book of Common Prayer* and the Bible have been in his bloodstream since childhood. His meditations on Scripture find physical expression through his hands, working first in clay and subsequently in bronze. Liz was brought up in the Evangelical tradition, where she was taught to have a daily quiet time with God and encouraged to meet with others to pray. She has explored different traditions of prayer over a long period of time and discovered the importance of engaging all our faculties in prayer — mind, body, spirit, the emotions and the imagination. She uses words constantly, writing, teaching, preaching, reading, listening to the chatter of a toddler. A quiet time with yet more words does not always permit any response at depth. Evangelicals are word-centred and this has sustained them and given them their identity. Using sculpture to evoke a response in prayer is not to replace words with something else, but to complement that part of the mind which responds to words.

Jesus used words all the time, but he painted pictures with words, used images from everyday life to explain his message and told evocative stories which made an impact deep within people's hearts. We have discovered that sculpture tells a story too.

Jesus painted pictures with words; we have discovered that sculpture tells a story too

What is Sculpture?

The immediately obvious difference between sculpture and other visual art is that it comes in three dimensions. But what is it?

The craft of sculpture is almost as old as time, and the lost wax process by which a bronze is made from a wax model is one of the oldest industrial processes known. It was practised by the Chinese long before the Egyptians made artefacts or Aaron's golden calf emerged from the fire (Exodus 32.24). Tubal-Cain (Genesis 4.22) is described as a craftsman who made bronze and iron tools; his name means instructor. Hiram, who worked on Solomon's temple, was a master craftsman and the son of a man from Tyre who was a 'worker in bronze' (1 Kings 7.13).

In the New Testament, Demetrius the silversmith stirred up a riot in Ephesus against Paul and his fellow members of the Way (Acts 19.21–41). As their skills were channelled into making idols, they were likely to lose trade and livelihoods when faced with the living God.

The Old Testament prophets and psalmists taunted the makers of idols: 'They have mouths but do not speak; eyes, but do not see' (Ps 115.5, see also vv 3–8). 'Those who make them are like them; so are all who trust in them' (v 8).

Isaiah 44.9–20 mocks the craftsman who fashions an idol from one end of a block of wood and burns the other end to keep warm (compare Isa 46.5–7; Jer 10.1–10; also the book of Wisdom 15.7–17).

Sculpture has played an important part in ancient history, as assets for the hereafter in the tombs of the Egyptian Pharaohs, or as records of the deeds and military campaigns of Nebuchadrezzar and Ashurbanipal of Assyria. Some of these may be seen in our national museums. The terracotta armies of ancient China hit the news some years ago and drew large crowds to see them, while thousands continue to visit our great cathedrals, if not to pray, then to wonder at the art and architecture found there, of which sculpture is a significant element.

Occasionally a modern sculpture hits the headlines. Anthony Gormley's *Angel of the North* towering over the city of Gateshead, has drawn both scorn and admiration. The sculptor represented in these pages draws the line at unmade beds, unless the whole has been moulded and cast in bronze! A large proportion of his sculptures are portrait heads, begun in clay with the sitter in front of him. They are statements by one person about another which can be handed on to future generations—if the sitter likes what he or she sees!

Sculpture is sometimes a prime source of self-expression in three dimensions, whether of someone short-lived like Henri Gaudier-Brzeska (visit Kettle's Yard, Cambridge) or the full life of someone like Picasso. The latter's vast output is like a great wheel where the rim is the continuity of a human story and the spokes are different avenues of expression from the hub which is the man himself.

> We need to learn to place ourselves in the shoes of others, and see things from other perspectives

Sometimes, as in all art, we do not know how much or what the sculptor believed about God. Yet he or she can still speak to us and challenge us to see the world through another's eyes.

Rodin's *Gates of hell* are as much a commentary on life and faith as Michelangelo's *Pieta* or Donatello's *David*. We need to learn to place ourselves in the shoes of others, and see things from other perspectives so that we can better appreciate our own. It is also vital that we do this in order to communicate the gospel to people whose outlook on the world is different from ours. Art can help us to do this. Sculptors worth looking out for are Michelangelo (15/16th century), Bernini (17th century), Rodin (19th/20th century), Elizabeth Frink (20th century) and Jacob Epstein (20th century).

You might like to make a conscious effort to seek out some sculpture near you. Parish churches are a good place to start. Many town centres have a sculpture or two, and public buildings are another place to find them. Look at them carefully, noting what you see in front of you, what your reactions are, and whether they evoke any other, apparently random, associations for you. Touch them if you can.

A Quiet Day with Sculpture

The quiet days we led using sculpture were set up as follows. We arranged a number of sculptures in pairs around the allotted space, preferably in different rooms. There was no title indicated on any of the sculptures. After an introduction on prayer and using our God-given imagination, people were let loose, Bible in hand, with the sculptures. They were given considerable time just to sit and look and touch if they wanted to do so. They were encouraged to let their minds range freely over the Scriptures and see if any passage or story or verse was suggested by the sculpture before them. It was suggested that they might come up with their own title to describe their feelings and match a Bible passage of their choice. It could also be a mood or feeling which was suggested, which in turn might lead to a particular part of the Bible. People could stop there and move on to a different sculpture, or they could do a word study, write their own story, poem or meditation or simply sit in silence with their chosen image. Afterwards we came together and shared what we had discovered. At the end, and only after everyone had said what they felt for themselves, the sculptor described what he was trying to do in each instance. Sometimes someone had already read his intention in a particular bronze and that was okay. At other times something completely different had suggested itself and that was okay too. Art, like Scripture, speaks to us in many ways according to our state of mind and heart and external circumstances.

Art, like Scripture, speaks to us in many ways according to our state of mind and heart and external circumstances

The Imagination in Prayer

You are probably familiar with how a visual image works in directing our thoughts Godwards, perhaps without having analysed it too deeply. You are out walking in the countryside. The air is fresh and clean, the birds are singing, you turn a corner and the view before you causes your own heart to sing a prayer of praise and thanksgiving to the loving creator. You remember the psalmist who sang 'The heavens are telling the glory of God...'

Or you meet someone and talk to them, and when you part, the expression on their face stays with you. Perhaps it was a face full of pain and sorrow and reminded you of someone in the Scriptures who cried out to God in anguish, and you lift them to God in prayer—'Jesus, son of David, have mercy.'

Christians have often been suspicious of the imagination. It can all too easily run away with us and lead us into areas where we do not wish to trespass. We live in a visual age and are used to having our eyes bombarded with images from every imaginable quarter. While this lays us wide open to unhealthy associations, there is a right use of these God-given faculties. Our eyes and our imaginations need sanctifying as much as the rest of us, but we need not assume that they give the Holy Spirit any more trouble than our other faculties. Moreover, a healthy use of them could help them to blossom as our creator intended.

Poetry has as much a place in the communication of God's truth as facts

If the record of the Bible is anything to go by, then poetry has as much a place in the communication of God's truth as facts. Sculpture, like poetry, is an art form which relies on allusion, metaphor, imagery and occasionally paradox. Yet there is still the same attitude around as that of Mr Gradgrind in Dickens' *Hard Times*: 'Stick to facts, sir!' So, yes, the writers of Scripture used plenty of facts, but they also used story and poetry, allegory, alliteration, and many other literary devices which invite the imagination to go to work. Jesus and Paul were both poets. When Jesus talked about the kingdom of God he did not give a list of plain facts with which we could define it. Rather, he alluded to it in picture language. Likewise, looking at sculpture as we suggest here is an invitation to imagine how things are and, if we will, to move on to imagine how things might be. The comments of other viewers show the diversity of the imagination when it is connected with real life. Some of the comments appear to contradict each other or cancel one another out because the images evoked a response according to what the viewer was experiencing at the time. It was the same when Jesus originally told his stories. We are so used to being told what each story means that we tune out our personal response to the different elements of the story. We do not allow them to work their power deep within us and so their impact is weakened. If only we could hear them again for the first time, as something fresh and new...

As for the contradictory nature of some of the comments, listen to the paradox of the gospel in the juxtaposition of language in the apostle Paul in one of his most rhetorical passages: 'Impostors yet true,/Unknown, well known,/dying, living,/sad, happy,/poor, wealthy,/destitute, abundant' (2 Cor 6.8–10). The juxtaposition of language here points to the mystery and immensity of the Christian life as well as the facts.

Some of the sculptures are taken from life models while others are composites or arise directly from the sculptor's imagination. The latter has been nourished by close observation of ordinary things—a man going home in the cold and wet, men and women at work, mothers and children. Emotions, feelings and moods somehow have to be translated into clay or bronze. What is going on as the hands of the sculptor mould and shape the clay? What is he trying to convey and how can he do it? Sculpting is an art which embraces more than just the practical skill of the one sculpting. It demands the whole attention in the making. And not just attention, but mind and heart, emotions and imagination and physical effort. Bronze is very heavy! If the creation of a work of art demands so much from its creator, then we as the onlookers might expect to have some demands made upon us too.

Using the Senses

Life involves a challenge to think, care, eat, drink, laugh, play, enjoy, converse, believe, pray, love, create, do and experience this amazing world in which we live. It is very easy, however, not to take time to step back and reflect on what is happening to us and around us. Looking closely at the sculptures depicted here will take time if we are to begin to reflect.[3] We are observing something closely simply in order to see what is there. As we look we are allowing ourselves to make connections with our own experience, our knowledge and understanding of God and the Christian life, and to respond. We are raising our awareness through the use of our senses.

We are mainly concerned with sight here, but try to involve your other senses too. What do you hear as you look at the sculptures? Does it evoke a memory of a smell? Or taste? Touch has a central place. You cannot touch the sculptures reproduced in this booklet, but a lot of sculpture is intended to be touched as well as viewed with the eyes. Gardeners often say how they like to feel the soil between their fingers. Mostly, however, we fail to notice what we touch. People on the London Underground pressed together are not consciously aware of all the different textures touching them. In our privileged world where water is available at the touch (!) of a tap, we wash our hands without noticing the feel of the water on our skin. On the other hand, inappropriate touching is high on our agenda. Sadly we have become almost paranoid where touch is concerned, and now legislate to prevent it happening.

Touch is one of the five senses which we rely upon every day. It protects us and informs us about our environment. It can also give great pleasure: a warm soft towel following a bath, a new baby's tiny finger, the intimate touch between a loving couple.

Using these bronze sculptures in quiet days has involved an invitation to touch and feel the figures in front of us. Indeed one of the first questions people ask is 'May I touch?'

You might wish to try a simple exercise to raise your awareness of touch.

Ask someone to place some objects inside a bag so that you cannot see them. Pick one out and explore it with you eyes shut. Describe what you can feel in as many words as you can and make comparisons and associations.

Another simple exercise is to wander round your house touching items you usually pass by without a second glance. Close your eyes and 'see' with your hands what is in front of you.

Sculpting Prayer and Praying Sculpture

We offer these meditations on prayer and sculpture in the hope that readers will themselves participate in the adventure of prayer. We suggest that you read the booklet with a piece of blank paper beside you. Cover up the comments which follow each image and take time to look at the picture of the sculpture first of all. Allow ten minutes and jot down any thoughts that come to mind — moods, memories, emotions, events — and try to relate the image to Scripture passages. Following the image are some comments made by others who have spent time with the sculptures, so it is important to let your own thoughts occur before reading these. Here is an invitation to allow your imagination free flight. In the same way that we sometimes avoid silence by filling it with sounds, some people will want to avoid the empty space and move quickly on to more words. But in music, if you ignore the rests, the empty spaces where there are no notes, the whole rhythm is destroyed, the tune wrecked. 'Empty' spaces have an important part to play in the rhythm of our lives. Our senses are taking things in all the time, and much of it remains undigested.

'Empty' spaces have an important part to play in the rhythm of our lives

Sculpture, like all art, is intended to evoke a personal response. The image is like the opening of a conversation, a spiritual conversation, a talk without the need for closure. It is unlikely that someone goes away from engaging with these sculptures and forgets about them or about the things they have called to mind. Most likely the conversation will continue in another place; further thoughts will suggest themselves, another Bible passage perhaps, something to be done or said. The comments which follow the images should reinforce this sense of openness. They are wide-ranging in scope. They represent a sample of what others discovered through looking at the image in question. It is most important that the sculptures do not have titles for the first part of the exercise. This allows for the viewer to use his or her imagination rather than be guided by someone else, even though that someone might be the artist. All too often we look at a work of art, read the title and stop looking. A friend was once visiting my home and saw a picture hanging on the wall. 'I don't like that picture,' she said. 'Oh,' I replied, 'it's called "The last swallow of summer."' 'Then I do like it,' she immediately responded! We have included fewer comments for the later images so as to encourage you to do your own thinking.

A face can suggest a dozen different thoughts and emotions. Some will like the image they see before them. They will immediately be stimulated to embark on an imaginative journey of associations. Other images will disturb. Maybe they are touching something deep within us which we usually ignore. It is very important to stay with the image long enough to go beyond our initial thoughts and feelings and to hear with the ear of the heart. We need to press beyond knee-jerk reactions for God is always drawing us deeper. Scripture can help us here. We may be surprised at what comes into our head. Relating it to a verse of Scripture or biblical story may be the key to allowing God to speak to us through the image. Some of the sculptures will take longer than others to stimulate thought and imagination. Allow whatever time it takes for the image to make an impact.

Having given yourself enough time to allow words and images to suggest themselves to you and to make connections with Scripture, you may find that your response to the sculpture takes on a creativity of its own. You may find your thoughts turning into poetry, for example. You may want to get out some paint and create a picture. The

You may find that your response to the sculpture takes on a creativity of its own

images in the booklet are made from bronze, a single colour. You may want to respond to this with a riot of colours. On the other hand, you may want to get hold of a piece of clay and make your own sculpture.

Praying with Sculpture Together

The original experience of these meditations was as a communal activity and there is great benefit in this. It is a reminder that the Bible is a communal book and intended to be interpreted that way. It is good to share our thoughts with other believers and be encouraged on our personal journeys. It is more difficult to do this with a booklet. You may like to obtain further copies and experiment with the sculptures together. There is still plenty of value, however, in doing this exercise alone and allowing the imagination free rein. Hopefully you will make some useful connections between the Scriptures and your own life; that is what this booklet is all about. Sculpture, like any other aid to prayer, is only helpful when it points us further along the road towards integrating knowledge of Scripture, experience of life and our encounter with the living God.

The other major difference between using this booklet and a quiet day with real sculptures is that on the quiet day you would be seeing them in three dimensions. A further difference is that the sculptures are depicted here in black and white. In reality the figures are all bronze in colour, but of course the daylight casts a variety of light and shade onto the metal, adding depth and movement.

You would notice the light and shade, the texture of the bronze, the flaws in the metal, the size and so on. You would be invited to touch the figures and allow this sense to feed your prayer. These pictures are two-dimensional and therefore more limited. They can still stimulate the imagination, however, and suggest Scriptures to you as you look. It is a beginning and may lead to a greater awareness of how art in general may nourish prayer and deepen our understanding of how God deals with us and speaks to us through his creation.

Why are the Figures Naked?

Toddy has always sculpted his figures unclothed for the simple reason that the body speaks more clearly when we can see it. Posture, gestures, the shape of muscle and sinew all communicate the essence of the person. Clothes muffle the communication. It is also a reminder that we are naked before God. We cannot hide from him, as Adam discovered in the garden.

Another reason for the absence of clothing is that its presence creates a distraction: 'Haven't the fashions changed?' 'Did they really dress like that?' We stop reading the body's own expression and concentrate on the outward appearance of things.

Thirdly, bodies are beautiful, and not just the model-shaped images of perfection paraded in our Western society. Their beauty is humbling to behold; they are God's sculpted imagination. We must keep sight of the fact that we are bodies as well as souls.

Images and Commentaries by Participants and Sculptor

2

Sculpture 1   Sculpture 2

Participants' Comments

Sculpture 1

Benjamin Britten: *War Requiem*; aristocrat; sophisticated; of today; rich young ruler years later; 'I wouldn't like him if I met him'; God created man; pensive; nobody's fool; enjoying life; crumbling of defences; God is; Jesus, therefore there is hope; blind but now I see; repentance.

Sculpture 2

Fool for Christ; clerical clown; 'Has anyone seen my collar stud?'; simplicity in face; fool—red blood on cheeks, or is it the cross?; deep perception; creativity; Francis of Assisi: 'Build my church.'

Sculptures 1 and 2 (together)

Faith and foolishness; happiness and sorrow; the fool says in his heart 'There is no God'; gentleness: I am your shepherd; father and son; compassion; Jesus saying, 'Mary'; cross on cheeks: soldier of Christ; youth and age; the serenity of forgiveness; Paul and Peter (Acts 9 and 12).

Sculptor's Comments

Sculptures 1 and 2: David Jenkins and Roly Bain

The head of David Jenkins aroused some of the most diverse responses among observers. How could there be so many opposing ideas: unhappy/enjoying life; the empty eyes of false wisdom/blind but now I see? Yet this is an image of a human face and our humanity is full of contradictions. It is the face of an older person and so the passage of time has etched a whole range of experiences into the face. It is also perhaps no surprise that a man who has stirred up such reactions by his theological pronouncements should echo the different responses to him in his image! (see 1 Timothy 3.1–17; 5.17–22).

This is an image of a human face and our humanity is full of contradictions

There is gravity and humour ('Has anyone seen my collar stud?'), and hopefully most people have a share of both. There is also the suggestion of different responses to God. Is he really thinking there is no God? Who are we to say?

One or two recognized who this was. Does it make a difference to our perceptions when we know, or think we know, what is going on? Where does prejudice creep in to the way we see how things are?

A lot of people liked the cross on Roly's cheek. It was immediately suggestive of Christian themes, and the connection with the clown image drew many to reflect on the idea of being a fool for Christ's sake. The clown also suggests play and humour. Many people associate religion with humourless solemnity and have never experienced the joyful freedom of knowing God in Christ. Perhaps they have not been helped by a church which has frowned on a lighthearted approach to life. In Jesus' words, however, we discover that the fullness of life he is offering sets us free from the things that would otherwise weigh us down.

In 1 Corinthians 1.18 Paul says, 'For the word of the cross is folly to those who are perishing, but to us who are being saved it is the power of God.' Watching Roly in the flesh, dressed in the traditional clown's garb and talking about the cross from a precarious slack rope, demonstrates powerfully the relationship between faith and foolishness (see also Rom 1.22; 1 Cor 4.10 and various references in Ecclesiastes).

Has putting your faith in Christ ever seemed folly when a more reasonable way suggested itself? Have you ever been made to feel foolish for admitting you are a Christian?

How much joy and gratitude is there in your life? How is it expressed?

Sculpture 3

Sculpture 4

Participants' Comments

Sculptures 3 and 4

Role of dogs in Bible; interdependence/one spirit; behind and before; shy and alert; 'In all thy ways acknowledge him'; 'Yoked with Christ'; trust and obey/obedience and loyalty (Deut 11.1); looking down; he will not turn his face from us or cast us aside; faithfulness and obedience; lead and guide; steadfastness: face set towards Jerusalem; journeying: trust in God; Ps 86 'Answer me for I am poor and needy'; two shepherds/lost sheep; the dog knows; dog forced forward; striving against the storm; relationships; veiled; direction and following; sheltering dog and moving forward; disillusioned? a change of course—the man stopped the dog.

Sculptor's Comments

Sculptures 3 and 4: Hi lorst and Going home

The energy of *Going Home* is internal and suggests struggle, while that of *Hi Lorst* (dialect for the command to the dog to go and seek out the quarry) is external, reaching out, pushing forward. Man and dog have a working relationship. They need each other. The working relationship recalls the fact that God has chosen to work out his purposes through human beings who are prepared to trust him and obey his call (Lk 11.28–30).

> *He looks intent on trudging forward, striving against the storm, or is it the metaphorical storm inside?*

The relationship between the man and his dog suggested many ideas and images which mirror our relationship with God. Most people who own a dog talk of its faithfulness and even friendship. In this context it is the dog which speaks to us of God rather than the human figure, but in the sculptures it is the man who is in control and the dog who either sets off to do his bidding or follows faithfully home. Both sculptures indicate a strong and close relationship between two creatures.

In the sculpture *Going Home* the man has his coat closely to his face to protect him from the elements and is hunched against the wind and rain. He looks intent on trudging forward, striving against the storm, or is it the metaphorical storm inside? Churchill spoke of depression as a black dog at one's heels (compare Matt. 11.28–30).

Sculpture 5   Sculpture 6

Participants' Comments

Sculpture 5

Magnificat; Mary; Elizabeth awaits Mary; 'The babe leapt in her womb...'; 'the babe within leapt for joy...'; Ps 139: 'you created my inmost being...' 1 Cor 13.11; Jer 1.5: Chosen from the womb; expectancy/waiting; await Jesus Christ: 1 Cor 1.7; push out bump with pride...simplicity; older mum expectant—joy; Sarah: pregnant at last; 'Just as I am'; hope for the future; hard work: the fifth child! awaiting someone coming home; lady in waiting.

Sculpture 6

Compassionate love; unconditional love; 'I and the Father are one.'; Isaiah 49: 'The Lord called me from the womb...'; Isaiah 66.13: Comfort; 'Suffer the little children'; Hannah with Samuel; Jesus found in the temple; male and femaleness of God; 'underneath are the everlasting arms'; comfort and forgiveness; protection in a place of fear; visiting; Jesus weeps over Jerusalem: mother hen; care for the vulnerable; widow of Nain: son reborn; eastern man—God the father; 'This is my beloved Son...'

Sculptor's comments

Sculpture 5: With Child

The image naturally suggests the nativity of Jesus, but birth is a recurrent theme throughout the Bible, from Genesis to the rebirth of creation in Revelation.

This was made as a maquette of a pregnant woman, done as a study for a figure for a life-size panel: 'Jesus encounters the women of Jerusalem,' one of eight 'Stations of the Cross.'[4] The sculptor depicted the women of Jerusalem as a mother and toddler group.

A number of women followed Jesus to the cross, weeping with sorrow as they went (Luke 23.27–31). Jesus addressed them as 'Daughters of Jerusalem' saying 'Do not weep for me but for yourselves and for your children. For behold the days are coming when they will say: Blessed are the barren, and the wombs that never bore…' Thus there is sense of foreboding and sadness mingled with the expectancy and joy of approaching birth which some observers noticed in the sculpture. Most women, especially if it is their first birth, will be aware of an element of apprehension as well as joyful anticipation as they await the onset of labour.

Waiting can be hard work. There is a strong tradition in Scripture of people having to wait for God to speak or act: 'How long, O Lord?' Weariness can begin to take over, doubts creep in, yet faith will cling on that there will be an outcome. The image of Elizabeth awaiting the visit of Mary with her sense of hope for the future, or Sarah 'pregnant at last,' her long wait finally rewarded, is an encouragement to keep going when the light of faith has grown feeble. Hidden in the womb there is new life about to burst forth which will make all that waiting worth the while (see Lk 1.39–50; 2.5).

Sculpture 6: Mother and child

The child melts into the mother. The mother is sanctuary, and young children find here security and comfort. It is the idea of two figures making one shape which may not be physically possible, but which reads well and so conveys feeling. The nativity stories in both Matthew and Luke were also in mind here.

Sculpture 7

Sculpture 8

Participants' Comments

Sculptures 7 and 8

Adam and Eve: expulsion; 'Awake my soul'; anguish: anger and loss; Ps 137: By the rivers of Babylon; female: shame and defiance, open but hidden; him: open grief, full frontal; Lamentations of Jeremiah; female: Jerusalem sinned…her nakedness; male: passerby, see my sorrow; arms = cross; female: denial; male: accepting; let this cup pass from me; strength from prayer; female: fear of the Lord; Proverbs: the good wife—honour; eve of the wedding; submission; husband and wife *in extremis*; he's seen the light, she has not; defensive: Prodigal/Judas/woman taken in adultery; Psalm 22; male: stoning of Stephen; desperation: 'Lord forgive…'; make peace with God; shocked at revelation.

Sculptor's Comments

Sculptures 7 and 8: His grief on Thursday and Her grief on Friday

These two figures are maquettes for life-size figures. His grief in Gethsemane: 'Remove this cup from me; yet not my will but yours be done' (Luke 22.42). Luke tells us that his sweat was like great drops of blood falling on the ground (Lk 22.44). The arms crossed foreshadow the cross. Is he rising to the occasion demanded of him, even anticipating rising to new life? There is also a hint of Peter's despair after his denial of Jesus (John 18.15–22) and Judas' remorse after his betrayal of Jesus (Matt and Acts 1.18), as the position of the arms reflects the cross. Even Jacob wrestling in Genesis 32 is echoed here, though he has been specifically tackled in a sculpture in its own right.

Her grief is at the foot of the cross; the figure is about to collapse in despair. Mary Magdalene is more in mind than Jesus' mother Mary, for it is a lover's grief rather than that of a mother. There is no anticipation of the object of her grief being restored; she clings to God (see Matt 26.36–46 and parallel refs).

Think about how we express emotion physically. How do you show joy through your body? Or sorrow?

Sculpture 9   **Sculpture 10**

Participants' comments

Sculptures 9 and 10

Emerging; humility; vulnerability; 'I offer up my life in spirit and in truth'/self-offering; 'All that I have, all that I am is yours'; rebirth; despair...change; hope comes out; overcome by despair; John 16 'weep and mourn,' grief to joy; 'Daughters of Jerusalem do not weep...'; total; revelation—process of worship; worship demands we undress before God...; Isaiah 9.6 sorrow; Psalm 22; woman who anointed Jesus feet: humility; Rev 18: 'Fallen is Babylon the Great'; Genesis 1 and 2: Eve coming to life; awakening; dawning into light; womb-like return to God; repentance at foot of cross; response to life outside/my own feelings: readiness.

Sculptor's comments

Sculpture 9: Moonlight Sonata

Rodin's Fallen Caryatid inspired the idea.[5] Whilst working from life, the model's need to rest from the pose inspired further variations, so the result was three separate studies. There is a sense of burden in the first, but this variation moves on to something more relaxed. Creation and Genesis were in mind, but also the Annunciation and the Magnificat. John 8.1–12 is also echoed.

Sculpture 10: Aerobics and Stretching Nude

Having done a stretching nude study and taken a cast, the same figure was used to express something else about female fitness. By twisting the figure rather like a child's Action Man or a Barbie doll, the idea of aerobics suggested itself.

Perhaps it is Bathsheba after bathing, enjoying her body and exercising it, unaware that David is watching with other ideas in mind.

Rahab restored is another way of looking at this sculpture (Heb 11.31).

Watching the Olympic gymnasts reminds us of the agility and grace of the human body. Many people like to keep fit almost to the point of obsession in some cases and our society's preoccupation with health and well-being is pursued with religious zeal. Yet there is an ambivalence towards the body as the eating disorders anorexia and bulimia indicate, and as many people's comments about themselves reveal.

> What is your reaction to the nakedness of these two figures?
>
> The sculptor in this case offers a number of possibilities which could have influenced him. Does this disturb you? Would you prefer to have a clearly defined meaning?

Sculpture 11

Participants' Comments

Sculpture 11

Four lepers; does long life bring understanding? Job and his three comforters; 'Thy will be done'; without light they grope their way in darkness; why four?; breaking out/breaking free; something emerging; John: 'If you continue in my words....disciples...the truth will make you free'; heaviness/burden; Ps 18: the cords of death; Psalm 22: mocking Jesus; Ecclesiastes: an evil under the sun; foundation of faith on the rock; 'Look to the rock from which you are hewn'/rock of ages; four suggests resurrection; puzzlement; four individuals searching for God: four responses—apprehensive, recoiling, rejection, resigned; four apostles/evangelists; four gospel writers; two harmony, two discord; in God's image; survivors of the wilderness.

Sculptor's comments

Sculpture 11: The Transfiguration

Here is a group of four figures where each can be moved to create different juxtapositions and tensions. They are a combination of Jesus and three disciples who in turn become Jesus, Moses and Elijah with an onlooker, so one is often looking in a different direction or at a different angle.

You will see from the comments above that it also provoked the most wide-ranging comments, some diametrically opposed to each other. It is the most abstract of the sculptures which allows for a wide interpretation.

The group is a maquette, a starting point for a bigger sculpture.

Since the incident falls between a mention of death and resurrection, (Matt 17.1–8; Mk 9.2–13; Lk 9.28–36 and see verses before and after) it is poignant that the group can be moved about to say something new or be seen afresh. This sculpture, especially, invites us to handle the figures, move them about, allow them to say different things to us.

The Transfiguration event contains many themes: the sheer mystery of it all; the reaction of the disciples; the revelation of Jesus and God's affirmation of him; the command from heaven; glory. The theme of transfiguration is fundamental to Christian thinking and gives strength, hope and courage to go on to many people whose situations seem difficult or earthbound. What does it mean to you (2 Pet 1.17–19)?

What is your reaction now to these semi-abstract figures? Would you like to rearrange the figures? How do you imagine the Transfiguration? Where would you place yourself in the biblical scene?

Sculpture 12   **Sculpture 13**

Participants' Comments

Sculptures 12 and 13

Torso; body; poser; no identity; movement; 'Look out, here I am!' solid; dependable and reliable; dancer; powerful; a long way to go; striking; '…and God made man…and woman'; Genesis 1 and 2; Goliath; defiance; daring; poise.

These two sculptures are unusual representatives of male and female types. Do they open up new dimensions for you regarding the human frame? Movement is common to both and to the sculptor the Holy Spirit has always been suggestive of movement. How would you depict the movement of the Spirit?

Sculptor's Comments

Sculptures 12 and 13: L'homme qui Marche and Catwalk

A study by Rodin for his *John the Baptist* prompted the maquette for *L'homme qui Marche*. It has its own story. It is a very early post-art school work modelled in wax direct and cast into bronze. It was stolen from a gallery and mysteriously returned after five years. Additionally, if you place both feet on the floor as suggested, it is impossible to walk like that! Despite this it suggests movement as the eye travels up one leg and down the other. It is suggestive of biblical references to John the Baptist in the New Testament, but also Isaiah, walking a straight and level path, and being on our pilgrimage or spiritual journey.

Every paper we open seems to carry a fashion page. *Catwalk* is a model 'strutting her stuff.' Someone remarked how masculine her walk appears and was gratified to discover that female models are coached by men to walk in a particular way to make their impact. Again the body—and this time with clothing—becomes a shape to play with like fashion itself.

'Vanity of vanities,' said the preacher in Ecclesiastes.

<table>
<tr><td>Sculpture 14</td><td>Sculpture 15</td></tr>
</table>

Sculpture 14

Sculpture 15

Participants' Comments

Sculpture 14

Child thinking; contemplation; looking; meditation; Ps 131.2: 'as a child I have quieted myself'; innocence; trust; 'unless you become as children…'; Is 11.6: 'a little child shall lead them'; 'Let the children come to me'; 'When I was a child I spoke as a child'; Lk 1.80: 'the child grew and became strong.'

Sculpture 15

Eph 6: 'Put on the whole armour of God'; knight in armour; charge; defender of the faith; disguised; weapons against the evil one; peace not war; the shield of faith.

Sculptor's Comments

Sculpture 14: Briony

Henry Moore said that sculpture should be tight. In other words, a fist makes a better sculpture than an open hand because it is compact. *Briony* here is compact: a little girl sitting on her hunkers. It was done at a craft fair as a study.

Jesus said, 'Suffer the little children to come to me.' In many ways the church is still trying to come to terms with Jesus' acceptance of children. Spirituality and the freedom of expression within a child speaks for itself. This appeal is much used in other references of Jesus to the kingdom, for example, 'Unless you become as a child you cannot enter the kingdom of God.' This is part of the baptism service, where Jesus and Nicodemus are quoted (John 3). The state of mind is the key. It must be completely trusting and wholehearted like any child. There is also a delightful absence of self-consciousness in children. They are at home in their own bodies, comfortable with themselves.

> Are children naturally spiritual? Can you identify with this picture of trust and freedom?
> What does it say to the child in you?

Sculpture 15: Knight

The idea here is Paul's admonition in Ephesians 6 to 'put on the whole armour of God.' The knight is kitted out in full armour, every part of him covered. He is ready for anything. He is on the attack, rather than defence, fighting against evil. John Bunyan's hymn comes to mind: 'Who would true valour see, let him come hither.'

This knight represents something which is deeper than the Quixotic.

> Does the image of the knight in armour immediately speak to you of spiritual things? Earlier heroic cultures have depicted Christ as the true knight, while our own is often uncomfortable with military imagery. Does seeing an image like this help or hinder our perception?

3

Further Reading

M Levy, *The Human Form In Art* (Odhams, 1961)

K Clark, *The Nude* (Pelican, 1956)

P Seddon, *Gospel and Sacrament: Reclaiming a Holistic Evangelical Spirituality* (Grove Spirituality booklet, S 89)

You might like to organize a quiet day using sculpture for you own church group. You could find your own works of sculpture, or use other objects for the same purpose. We are also available to lead such a day for you using our own materials.

Contact: the Revds Hoare: tel 01845 537277

email: liz@lizhoare.wanadoo.co.uk

Notes

1   Trevor Dennis, *Imagining God: Stories from Creation to Heaven* (SPCK, 1997) ch 2.

2   See for example, *Who was Jesus?* (SPCK) and *What Saint Paul Really Said* (SPCK, 1997).

3   Another recent Grove booklet, available as an e-book, also helps us to develop the art of really seeing something as we look: David Runcorn, *The Creation of Adam* (Grove Spirituality booklet, S 76).

4   A maquette is a working study in the round to enable the sculptor to grasp the concept of an idea and make adjustments or variations.

5   Caryatids were female figures used as supporting columns in classical architecture.